The Visionary Leader

Leader Behavior Questionnaire — Self

Revised

Marshall Sashkin, Ph.D.

HRD P

Amherst, Massachus

The Visionary Leader
Leader Behavior Questionnaire—Self
Revised

Copyright © 1984, 1985, 1990, 1995 by Marshall Sashkin, Ph.D.

Published by **Human Resource Development Press, Inc.**
22 Amherst Road
Amherst, MA 01002

(800) 822-2801

ISBN 0-87425-346-2

The Visionary Leader

Leader Behavior Questionnaire—Self
Revised Edition

Warren Bennis, Peter Drucker, and others have observed that leaders are people who do the right thing while managers are people who do things right. Both roles are essential for organizational success, yet they are very different in their requirements. *The Leader Behavior Questionnaire (LBQ)* is designed to help you learn how you go about performing aspects of these roles in your own work as a leader. Even if you are not currently in a leadership position, the *LBQ* can provide you with feedback regarding your leadership potential. In either case, the *LBQ* gives you an opportunity to discover some valuable information about your personal approach to the leadership process. You can then go on to make personal development plans so that you will be able to contribute more to the level of excellence in your organization. To gain still further insights you may wish to provide copies of the *LBQ*–Other to some of your associates, who would complete it and return it for scoring. The most important assessment you can make of your own leadership activity or potential, using the *LBQ*, is to compare your self–assessment with the perceptions that other more objective observers have of you.

On the next two pages you will see a questionnaire, consisting of fifty statements. Each statement describes a certain leadership behavior, characteristic, or effect that a leader might have on the organization. Read each statement carefully. Try to estimate just how true each statement is for you: completely, mostly, somewhat, a little, or not at all. Your task is to indicate how true each statement is as a description of you.

Please remember that the results will be helpful to you only to the degree that they are an accurate reflection of your actual behaviors, characteristics, and effects. Thus, it is to your benefit to respond as candidly as possible.

Following the questionnaire pages is the *LBQ* Response Form. You can simply remove the Response Form from the booklet; this will make it easier to respond to the statements as you read them. Follow the directions on the Response Form, which has two parts, one attached below the other. As you make your responses on the top sheet, they are automatically transferred to the Scoring Form underneath the Response Form. Do not separate the Response Form from the Scoring Form until you have responded to each of the fifty statements on the questionnaire and have been instructed in how to score your answers.

QUESTIONNAIRE

I . . .

1. pay close attention to what others say when we are talking.

2. don't always communicate clearly.

3. am extremely dependable.

4. show that I really care about other people.

5. worry a lot about the possibility of failing.

6. believe that what I do is important because of the impact of my actions on people's behavior and on achieving organizational aims.

7. find that some of the most significant aspects of my position are the little "perks" that demonstrate my importance to the organization and its members.

8. often consider how a specific action plan I've developed might be extended to benefit my entire organizational unit.

9. haven't generally been able to help the organization attain its goals.

10. encourage people to support their views and positions with concrete evidence.

11. have a hard time getting others to understand me clearly.

12. make points in strikingly clear and even unusual ways.

13. follow through on commitments.

14. don't always respect myself as a result of my actions.

15. avoid taking risks.

16. can see the effects of my actions.

17. believe that the advantage of having a position of authority is being able to get people to do as one wishes without pointless discussion or debate.

18. focus on clear short-term goals rather than being concerned with longer-range aims.

19. have been able to help this organization adapt to changing conditions.

20. act to reach goals rather than trying to keep things the way they are.

21. have a clear set of priorities.

22. sometimes don't notice how others feel.

23. often find it desirable to change or alter my position.

24. recognize others' strengths and contributions.

25. find ways to get people fully committed to new ideas and projects.

26. do what is called for but realize that my actions are not likely to make much of a difference.

27. show that the real value of power is being able to accomplish things that benefit both the organization and its members.

28. have a hard time explaining my long-range plans and goals to others in the organization.

29. have difficulty dealing with problems of conflict and coordination.

30. help others develop a shared sense of what is important to us in this organization.

31. literally grab people's attention to focus them on the important issues in a discussion.

32. communicate feelings as well as ideas.

33. avoid committing to a position, preferring to remain flexible.

34. know and can say exactly how I fit into this organization.

35. learn from mistakes, treating errors as opportunities for learning rather than as disasters.

36. act on the principle that no one person can make very much of a difference in how this organization operates.

37. seek power and influence in order to attain organizational goals that everyone agrees are important.

38. look for ways that the plans and programs I've developed in my own unit might be expanded to benefit the entire organization.

39. express and support a set of basic values about how people should work together in this organization to solve common problems and reach shared goals.

40. help others understand that there is often little we can do to control important factors in the environment.

41. find it difficult to get others' attention when speaking with them.

42. am able to get complicated ideas across clearly.

43. am someone people feel they can depend on.

44. show little concern for other peoples' feelings.

45. communicate excitement about future possibilities.

46. believe that I can make a difference to this organization.

47. want influence to create programs and attain organizational goals that will benefit everyone in the organization.

48. have plans for this organization that extend over a period of several years or longer.

49. contribute to the organization's effective operation in terms of adapting to changes, attaining objectives, and coordinating the work activities of individuals and groups.

50. encourage others to pursue their individual work goals and compete with their co-workers to see who is the best.

Interpretive Guide

Introduction

The *Leader Behavior Questionnaire* (*LBQ*) was developed to study, and to provide individuals with personal feedback about, a new approach to leadership. This approach is sometimes called "transformational leadership" and is often referred to as "visionary leadership," as well. That's why these materials are titled *The Visionary Leader*. Since the first version of the *LBQ* was developed, in the early 1980s, it has been used in hundreds of research studies designed to investigate new concepts of leadership. The *LBQ* has also been used by over 100,000 managers as a tool for developing a better understanding of leadership and improving their own leadership skills. By getting feedback about your own leadership behaviors, your leadership characteristics, and your effect on the organization as a leader, you can identify specific ways to increase your leadership effectiveness.

A Brief History of Leadership

The study of leaders is not new, going back at least to Plutarch and his biographies of great persons, written in the first century. While scientific research on leadership only began in the twentieth century, literally thousands of formal research studies have been carried out over the past seventy-five years.

The earliest studies, starting in the 1920s, assumed that effective leaders were born, not made, and set out to identify their special characteristics. This has been called the "great person" approach to leadership: find out what characteristics are shared by great leaders and then look for those factors when selecting leaders. About twenty-five years of research led to the conclusion that leaders are generally a bit smarter, a bit more outgoing, slightly more inventive, and even a little taller than the average. However, neither these nor any other traits stand out so much as to be clearly or strongly associated with leadership.

In the 1940s researchers turned their attention to what leaders do, instead of who they are. That work identified two essential aspects of effective managerial leadership. The first has to do with providing clear instructions and directions. This is often called *task-oriented* leadership behavior. The second centers on giving personal support and encouragement and, for that reason, is usually called *relationship-oriented* leadership behavior.

It seemed at first as though the puzzle of leadership had been solved; if everyone simply learned how to engage in these two types of leader behavior, and did so skillfully enough, then there would be no shortage of successful leaders. Unfortunately it wasn't that simple. While engaging in these two categories of behavior does seem to have some general positive benefit for supervisors and managers, further research demonstrated that just those benefits are quite limited. Supervisors able to exhibit high levels of both task- and relationship-centered behavior do tend to have fewer grievances and better attendance and turnover records as compared with other supervisors. However, displaying these behaviors does not ensure outstanding performance on the part of either followers or leaders.

Thus, the 1960s saw the development of what are called contingency theories of leadership. That is, if it's not *who they are,* and it's not *what they do,* perhaps effective leadership involves *doing the right thing at the right time.* The most widely-used of the contingency approaches was developed by two scholars, Dr. Paul Hersey and Dr. Kenneth Blanchard, who call their approach **Situational Leadership.** By using their model to assess the willingness and the capability of followers to do a job, a manager is able to determine what combination of task and relationship behavior will be most effective in a particular situation. Grounded in research, Situational Leadership was one of the first approaches that really gave managers a handle on becoming more effective leaders; it is probably now the most widely used management improvement approach in the world. (All of Paul Hersey's Situational Leadership materials are now available from HRD Press.)

Although Situational Leadership can make a difference when managers use it to guide their actions, it does not solve the puzzle of leadership. For one thing, it is far more applicable to the world of the first-level supervisor and mid-level manager than to the work of top-level leaders such as Bill Gates (co-founder of Microsoft) or Sam Walton (who founded Wal-Mart, now the world's largest retailer). It wasn't until James McGregor Burns, a political historian, turned his attention to the question of leadership that we began to make real progress in understanding its nature, operation, and development. As is often the case, it took someone from outside the world of management or management research to come up with truly new ideas, ideas that would break the old paradigm and lay the foundation for a new one.

For Burns, leadership has little to do with the work of the factory foreman. His concern for leadership centers on the work of the leaders of nations, people like Napoleon, Franklin D. Roosevelt (about whom Burns wrote a Pulitzer Prize-winning biography), Joseph Stalin, and Winston Churchill. Burns asked himself what it was about individuals considered great national or social leaders, especially people considered moral leaders, such as Mohandes Ghandi and Martin Luther King, Jr., that made them successful. In 1978 he published a book, simply titled **Leadership.** In this book Burns explains the difference between leaders who create visions that *transform* both followers and societies, and leaders who get followers to do as the leader wishes by means of a *transaction* — money, praise, or some other reward (or punishment). At best, these *transactional* leaders get what they expect, while *transformational* leaders get (as Dr. Bernard Bass later put it) performance *beyond* expectations.

This doesn't mean that transactional leadership is unimportant. In fact, it is crucial both for effective management and as a basis for transformational leadership. We noted earlier that managers do things right while leaders do the right things. Organizations need things done right to operate. And, they must have identified the right things to do, if operations are to continue over the long haul. Thus, organizations need both good management, for current operations,

and sound leadership to develop a long-term strategy. Effective management tools, like Situational Leadership, are important if managers — and those they work with — are to do things right. But doing things right isn't enough. If the wrong things are done it won't matter whether they were done right or not; the organization will fail. Without effective management nothing can be accomplished, but without effective leadership to help determine what *should* be accomplished, accomplishments may prove to be of little value.

The Visionary Leader

While Burns provided the initial ideas and impetus for our current understanding of transformational leadership, it was up to others to focus his ideas on business organizations (rather than nations or social movements) and to research those ideas. Visionary Leadership Theory brings together the concepts and research findings of many scholars and researchers, as they relate to transformational leadership. This work is organized in terms of three major aspects of transformational leadership: behaviors, personal characteristics, and organizational culture-building activities.

Transformational leadership behaviors. Work on the strategic behaviors of exceptional executives by Warren Bennis (at the University of Southern California) forms one of the behavioral foundations of the **LBQ**. In the early 1980s Bennis conducted in-depth interviews with ninety chief executives, in organizations of all sorts, including the leading manufacturer of office furniture, General Electric, the Girl Scouts of America, and a symphony orchestra. He identified a set of behavioral patterns characteristic of leaders who were successful and inspired their followers in a visionary manner. Bennis found that when leaders used these behaviors, their followers saw them as visionary, charismatic, and transformational. The first five scales of the **LBQ** assess the extent to which individuals engage in each of five visionary leadership behaviors similar to those identified by Bennis. The **LBQ** measures are also based on a set of very similar behaviors identified (independently of Bennis) by two researchers at the University of Santa Clara, Dr. James Kouzes and Dr. Barry Z. Posner. They used their results as the basis for their best–selling and influential book, *The Leadership Challenge*. The *LBQ* measures five specific behaviors quite similar to those identified by all of these researchers as common actions of effective transformational leaders.

These five behaviors are:

- Providing a clear focus on key issues and concerns, that is, on the right things;

- Getting everyone to understand this focus through effective organizational communication practices;

- Acting consistently, over time, so as to develop trust;

- Demonstrating through actions that they care for and respect the organization's members;

- Creating empowering opportunities that involve the organization's members in making the right things their own priorities.

We will discuss these five transformational leadership behaviors in more detail in a later section of this booklet.

Transformational leadership characteristics. Transformational leadership requires more than just a set of specific behaviors. Recall that while earlier research identified important behaviors, managers who engaged in those behaviors to a great extent were not necessarily the most successful leaders. Effective top–level leadership, transformational leadership, depends not only on an individual's behavioral skills but on certain characteristics. This may seem to contradict the earliest leadership research which was reasonably conclusive in rejecting the notion that some set of traits can be used to identify great leaders. But what we call characteristics are not the same as traits. That is, these characteristics are not fixed but can be developed. There are, in particular three important characteristics that transformational leaders must develop within themselves. Each has been studied by one or another group of researchers. Visionary

Leadership Theory, on which the *LBQ* is based, brings these together to show how they work in unison as the personal basis for transformational leadership. Each of the three personal characteristics is assessed by a scale of the *LBQ*.

The first of the three characteristics assessed by the *LBQ* is something so simple that it may seem obvious. Psychological researchers such as Dr. Albert Bandura, on whose work this leadership characteristic is based, sometimes make it sound terribly complex by calling it "self-efficacy" or "efficaciousness." It has even been referred to by the mysterious label "agency." But what "it" is is nothing more — or less — than *self–confidence*. The key is not simply self–confidence but its development. That is, we develop self–confidence through experience. In practice this most often means being encouraged to try to accomplish a task and then succeeding. Success is not, however, due to chance; the person encouraging one (often a transformational leader) usually feels certain that one can succeed. The person encouraging you may be a parent, a teacher, a coach, or a boss. Regardless, that person doesn't just spout glib homilies ("You can do it!"). He or she goes beyond that to guide, to teach, to provide the knowledge or practice needed to help you succeed. The more extensive this pattern of encouragement, effort, support, and success the stronger and more general becomes one's self–confidence. The self–confidence described is, then, no mere boast. It is a grounded belief in one's own ability to make a difference. It is a sense of assurance that what one does can have a real and meaningful impact.

The second crucial personal characteristic assessed by the *LBQ* is based on the work of Dr. David McClelland (of Harvard University) on the need for power. In an important study with Dr. David Burnham, published in the *Harvard Business Review,* they reported that effective leaders were driven not by the need to achieve (as they had expected) but by a need for power. Examining the data more closely, they found that while a high need for power was common to most mid– and higher–level managers, this need was *not* necessarily related to effective leadership. Individuals at these levels with high power needs were effective leaders only if that power need was directed in certain, positive ways. That is, effective leaders use power and influence to benefit the organization and its members, not just to satisfy their own desires or to benefit themselves. This sort of use of power is commonly referred to as *empowerment*. That is, power and influence is used not to make others do as the leader wishes but to empower others to use power and influence to accomplish meaningful tasks and attain important goals. Of course, power is not much good to a leader unless that person believes it can be used to make a difference, to have a positive impact. That's why the first characteristic, self-confidence, is so important.

The third personal characteristic tapped by the *LBQ* is derived from the work of Dr. Elliott Jaques, an organizational psychologist who has spent more than forty years studying the nature of vision in organizational leadership. From this groundwork Jaques constructed a new theory of cognitive development based on *time span*. This refers to how long and how complex a series of actions one can plan and think through. Effective visionary leaders who are CEOs of large organizations generally have vision spans of more than a decade. That is, they can think about and make plans, in meaningful detail, for complex projects that consist of many elements and activities occuring over a period of years. In contrast, a first-line supervisor might only think in terms of a few months. Jaques finds that time span can and does increase, sometimes dramatically, over a person's life span. One's current span is not a limitation, but can be used to determine if you are at the right organizational level at present, as well as to identify personal development needs.

The first five behavioral scales of the *LBQ* provide reliable measures of transformational leadership behavior. However, the three scales that measure transformational characteristics are not designed to give precise psychological assessments. These scales are intended to provide you with information for self-examination that will help you increase your self-understanding as a basis for personal development planning. The three characteristics are measured not as pure psychological traits but in terms of specific behaviors that indicate the presence and degree of that characteristic.

Transforming organizational culture. Dr. Edgar H. Schein, an organizational psychologist at the Massachusetts Institute of Technology, has written extensively on leadership and organizational culture. Schein contends that effective leaders design and develop productive organizational cultures. Indeed, he suggests that doing so may be the *only* really important task of leaders! An organization's culture consists of the enduring patterns of assumptions, beliefs, and values that are shared by its members. This does not mean that everyone carries around a written list of values and beliefs, for handy reference. Most of these shared values and beliefs are simply taken for granted and are rarely if ever openly referred to. They are carried around in our heads and our hearts and they are expressed in our every action. Sometimes organization members are unaware of important values and beliefs that shape their behavior.

The specific assumptions, values, and beliefs that support organizational effectiveness relate to four key organizational functions originally defined by an American sociologist, Dr. Talcott Parsons. These are: managing change, achieving goals, coordinating teamwork, and maintaining a strong organizational culture through widely shared assumptions, beliefs, and values. Parsons argues that these functions must be performed effectively by any organization that wishes to survive. It would be difficult to imagine how an organization could survive long without performing these functions.

Linking Parsons' work with Schein's, we can say that transformational leaders have positive effects on the key organizational functions by building strong cultures. They do this by instilling assumptions, values, and beliefs that support the four key functions. The final section of the *LBQ* assesses the extent to which leaders act to build cultures that help the organization carry out the four functions.

What the *LBQ* Measures

In summary, the *LBQ* yields three different sets of scores:

- the extent to which you use visionary leadership behaviors;

- the degree to which you possess the personal characteristics required of visionary leaders;

- the extent to which you have (or could have) a positive impact on your organization's culture.

The first five scales, measuring specific leadership behaviors, are designed to provide reliable and accurate assessments of your own behavior as it relates to transformational leadership. Scales six, seven, and eight assess personal characteristics. They form a second set of measures intended to spur self-understanding and help plan for self-development. The final two scales, nine and ten, are designed to give an indication of the extent to which you are (or are capable of) building a sound organizational culture.

How to Score the *LBQ*

The scoring of the *LBQ* is made easy by means of the pressure sensitive Response Form you have just completed. Separate the top sheet (the Response Form) from the bottom sheet (the Scoring Form). You will see that your marks on the Response Form have also circled numbers on the Scoring Form. If any circles are unclear, return to the top sheet to locate your original response and recircle the appropriate number on the Scoring Form. Add the circled numbers in each column of the Scoring Form and put the sum in the box provided for a Subtotal, at the bottom of each column.

If your associates have completed the *LBQ*–Other, these instruments should be scored in a like manner. (You may be provided with the ten subtotals for each associate rather than the actual scoring forms.) Assign a letter, A, B, C, D, or E, to each associate's instrument or set of scores. As you record the scores on this and the follwoing page

be consistent in entering all of the data from associate A into the boxes labeled A; do the same for each of the other associates giving you feedback.

Visionary Leadership Behavior Score

Add the totals for columns 1, 2, 3, 4, and 5. Put the sum in the Self box, on the left of the chart below. The remaining boxes are for scores provided by your associates. Add these scores across and divide the total by the number of your associates who responded. (Note: Do not include your Self score in the average.) The average of your associates' scores goes in the Others Average box, below. You may have been provided with only the average of your associates' scores, not with their individual responses. In that case, just enter the average in the final box on your right.

SELF	A	B	C	D	E	TOTAL OTHERS	OTHERS AVERAGE
79							

Visionary Leadership Characteristics Score

Add the totals for columns 6, 7, and 8. Put the sum in the Self box, below. The remaining boxes are for scores provided by your associates. Add these scores across and divide the total by the number of your associates who responded. (Note: Do not include your Self score in the average.) The average of your associates' scores should be placed in the final box.

SELF	A	B	C	D	E	TOTAL OTHERS	OTHERS AVERAGE
47							

Visionary Culture Building Score

Add the totals for columns 9 and 10. Put the sum in the Self box, below. The remaining boxes are for scores provided by your associates. Add these scores across and divide the total by the number of your associates who responded. (Note: Do not include your Self score in the average.) Place the average of your associates' scores in the final box.

SELF	A	B	C	D	E	TOTAL OTHERS	OTHERS AVERAGE
30							

Now place the Self scores and Others Average scores in the boxes provided for Visionary Leadership Behavior, Visionary Leadership Characteristics, and Visionary Culture Building on page 10.

Your Visionary Leadership Total Score

Transfer the three Self scores you just entered in the boxes above to the boxes below. Then add across for your Visionary Leadership Total Score—Self. Do the same for the three Others Average scores to produce a Visionary Leadership Total Score—Others.

	LEADER BEHAVIOR	LEADER CHARACTER	CULTURE BUILDING		
SELF	79	47	30	156	TOTAL SELF
OTHER					TOTAL OTHER

Enter the two Total scores in the boxes provided on the following summary score page. To obtain a visual representation of your Self score, place an "X" at the appropriate scale point along the mountain trail shown on the illustration; use an "O" to mark the Others Average score.

The five scoring ranges labeled on the next page are defined in the following chart:

Range	Interpretation
226–250	*At the summit.* You have a panoramic view of the countryside. On a clear day you can see forever.
201–225	*On the final ascent.* You are preparing for the last, crucial segment of your climb. You can see your goal, the peak, just ahead.
176–200	*At the snow line.* Through breaks in the trees you are able to glimpse the summit. The ascent ahead is clear in your view.
146–175	*On the trail up.* You can see the trail leading up and the base camp behind you. Some height will improve your vision.
50–145	*At the piedmont* (foothills). Your view is obscured at the base of the mountain by trees, shrubs, and rocks.

Are You A Visionary Leader?

Visionary Leadership Behavior Score

Self	Others' Average
79.	

Visionary Leadership Characteristics Score

Self	Others' Average
44	

Visionary Culture Building Score

Self	Others' Average
30	

Visionary Leadership Total Score

Self	Others' Average
156	

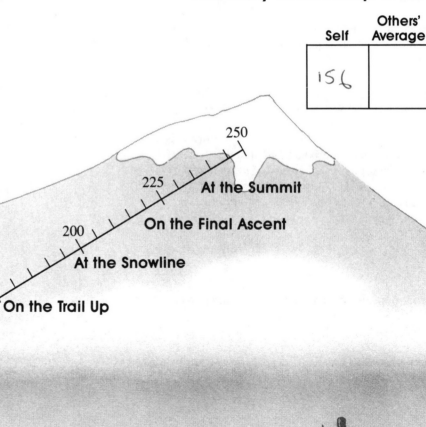

250 — At the Summit
225 — On the Final Ascent
200 — At the Snowline
175 — On the Trail Up
150
100 — At the Piedmont
50

Behavior, Characteristics, and Culture Building Scores

Enter your three Self scores on the scales in the triangle below labeled "Self." Make a dot or an "X" at the appropriate point on each scale. Then connect the three points, forming a smaller triangle within the larger one. Do the same for the three Others Average scores, using the triangle below labeled "Others Average." The larger your triangles, the closer is your own leadership approach to that of the visionary leader. You can also learn from the shape of the triangles, as illustrated and explained on the following pages.

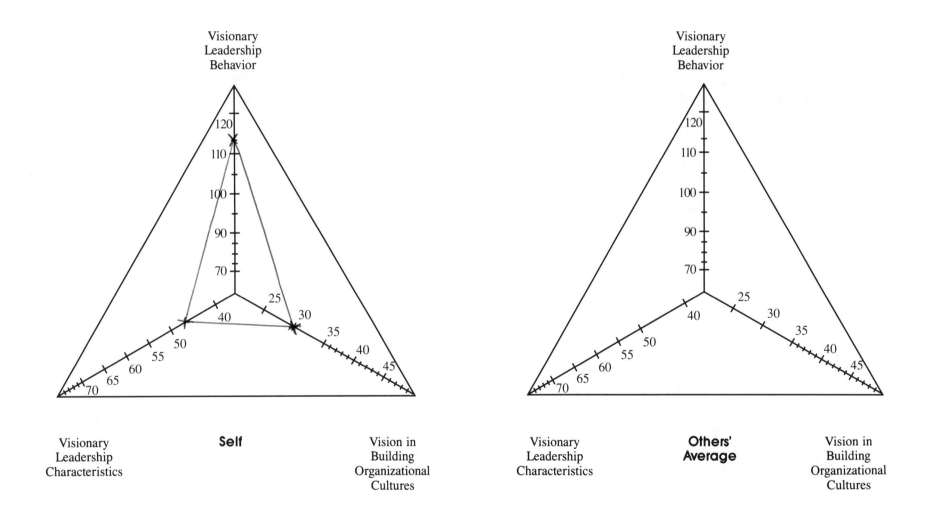

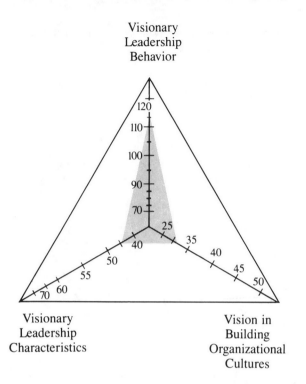

Visionary
Leadership
Behavior

Visionary
Leadership
Characteristics

Vision in
Building
Organizational
Cultures

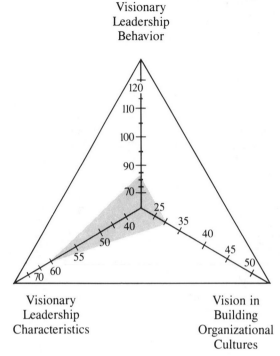

Visionary
Leadership
Behavior

Visionary
Leadership
Characteristics

Vision in
Building
Organizational
Cultures

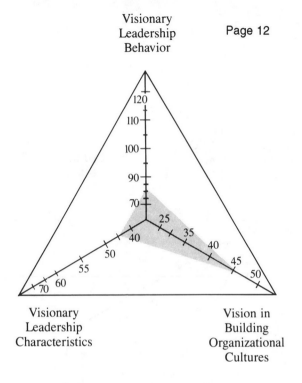

Visionary
Leadership
Behavior

Visionary
Leadership
Characteristics

Vision in
Building
Organizational
Cultures

The Charismatic Individual. This profile shows that the person is able to engage in the specific behaviors that visionary leaders use to get their visions across to followers. This individual, however, does not really have a clearly thought out vision, nor is there evidence that this person knows how and is able to build organizational culture, a crucial element of visionary leadership. Thus, the person with this profile comes across quite strongly — and probably positively — on an interpersonal level, but nevertheless is not acting as a visionary leader.

The Visionary Thinker. A person with this profile has great ideas and can see exactly how those ideas could become real in the organization. However, he or she lacks skills at the interpersonal and organizational levels that are needed to involve others and the organization in constructing a vision. The person may be convinced that the vision actually can be implemented, and may well realize the importance of empowering others to become owners of the vision. He or she is not, however, able to act on this understanding to implement a vision.

The Organizational Tinker. This profile describes an individual who might be seen as a "fixer," a person who knows the ins and outs of the organization and its politics. He or she knows how to manipulate organizational circumstances to get what he or she wants, and might even be seen as a model, as someone who typifies the values and beliefs of those in the organization and acts in ways consistent with the norms of behavior in the organization. Alternatively, this person might be seen as a "tinker," someone who is skilled in making minor repairs of a utilitarian sort, who knows how to make adjustments that keep things working — at least for a while. But this person has neither an organizational vision nor the interpersonal skills needed to implement a vision.

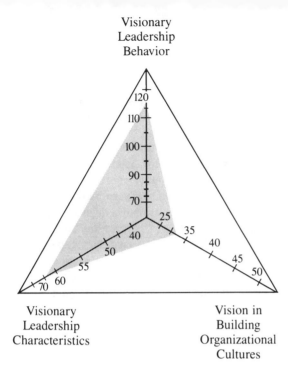

Visionary
Leadership
Behavior

Visionary
Leadership
Characteristics

Vision in
Building
Organizational
Cultures

The Visionary Charismatic. The person with this profile truly can be said to have both a vision and the interpersonal skills to communicate that vision to others, to enlist followers, and even to recruit "true believers" or disciples. What the visionary charismatic lacks, however, is an organizational understanding and the skills needed to build a vision into an organization's culture. This person's followers will always remain individuals, perhaps with a personal commitment to the leader but no such commitment to the organization. This limits the organization's capacity to develop a shared vision.

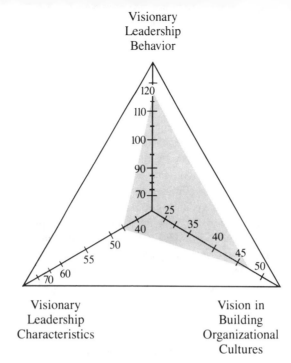

Visionary
Leadership
Behavior

Visionary
Leadership
Characteristics

Vision in
Building
Organizational
Cultures

The Organizational Architect. This individual has the behavioral skills to inspire and develop followers and build the organization's culture. This person, however, lacks the ability (or fails to understand the need) to develop an organizational vision. He or she may also be uninterested in power and influence, failing to understand that it is only through the use of influence that people work together to accomplish goals in an organization. An organizational architect may have a strong desire for personal power, for domination over others, rather than a desire to empower others to become owners of a shared vision. It is even possible that despite having exceptional skills this person doesn't believe that he or she can have a real impact on the organization. This individual may be personally effective, but is not acting in a way that involves either a vision or top–level leadership.

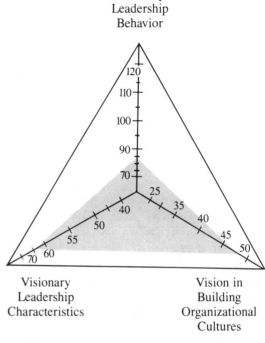

Visionary
Leadership
Behavior

Visionary
Leadership
Characteristics

Vision in
Building
Organizational
Cultures

The Organizational Planner. A person with this profile has a vision. He or she can see how that vision might be instilled within the organization, in terms of policies and programs, and the shared values and beliefs on which they are based. This individual, however, does not have the interpersonal skills needed to communicate a vision to others, to excite others, interest them, and ultimately empower them to buy into — and own — the vision. This individual may have an impact on the organization, through effective policy implementation and program development. These factors may even support elements of this person's vision. Still, the vision itself cannot be realized when organization members are not directly involved and empowered to take a strong and active role in making the vision real. That is only achieved by the direct interpersonal actions of a visionary leader.

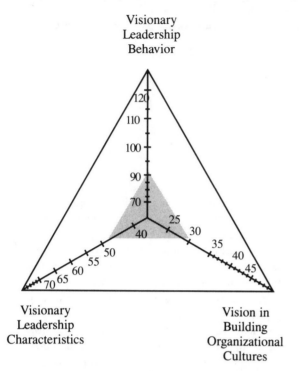

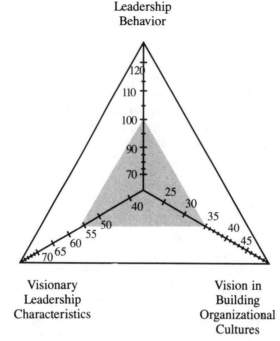

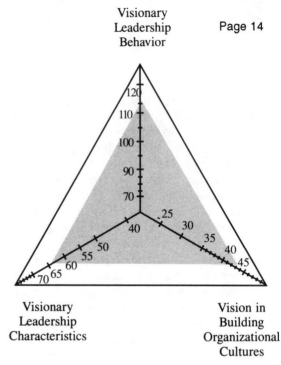

Visionary
Leadership
Behavior

Visionary
Leadership
Characteristics

Vision in
Building
Organizational
Cultures

Visionary
Leadership
Behavior

Visionary
Leadership
Characteristics

Vision in
Building
Organizational
Cultures

Visionary
Leadership
Behavior

Visionary
Leadership
Characteristics

Vision in
Building
Organizational
Cultures

The Underdeveloped Manager. With this balanced profile no matter which direction one picks there is a clear path to personal development. While there are no strong imbalances to overcome, one must first determine whether the job calls for management or leadership. If the answer is management, the next step is to assess one's managerial effectiveness (perhaps using the Situational Leadership approach) and make plans for developing those skills. If the position is one in which leadership is required and if the person is already a good manager, the first action would be to raise one's awareness of the nature of leadership, as distinct from good management. The next step would be to consider leadership development planning, beginning with a focus on the three personal characteristics required for effective visionary leadership.

The Aspiring Leader. The person with a profile that is average in each of the three areas of visionary leadership is in an excellent position for growth and development. Like the underdeveloped manager, this person is not overly focused on any one area. Moreover, the aspiring leader is likely to have sound managerial capabilities and to already be looking toward the challenge of leadership. This person may be feeling a degree of frustration, having some idea of what he or she is reaching for but not seeing a clear path to that goal. Often the strategy is to try even harder as a manager, but this only produces more frustration. Visionary leadership calls for actions quite different from those needed for effective management. Personal awareness of the nature of leadership should be the first action step.

The Self-Actualizing Leader. This ideal profile is unusual; very few people will have extremely high scores across the board. Such scores are strong evidence that one is currently acting as an effective leader. Research shows that individuals in responsible positions, who score quite high on all three *LBQ* subscales, have employees who report a high quality of work life, as well as high productivity and bottom-line outcomes. Leaders in this group are self-actualizing. But self-actualizing does not mean perfect! Even those who do score high on each of the three areas are likely to find that their scores on one or another of the scales that make up each of the three subscores indicate that there is room for improvement.

Interpreting Your *LBQ* Scores

As we used the metaphor of mountain climbing to help interpret overall *LBQ* scores, the following ranges and descriptions for each of the three sets of scores are intended to help interpret your subscores in more detail. The imagery of the interpretive phrases below is intended to suggest movement by leaders from the bases of their "mountains" to the "peaks," where greater clarity of vision is possible.

	Visionary Leadership Behavior Scores		Visionary Leadership Characteristic Scores
Range	**Interpretation**	**Range**	**Interpretation**
113–125	You have reached the peak by exercising the action skills of a professional mountaineer.	68–75	Your sight and fortitude have enabled you to empower your team to reach the peak.
102–112	On the final ascent you are using all your skills to communicate your vision of the peak and to empower your team to attain it.	60–67	You are developing in your team the will and vision that will enable them to take responsibility for reaching the goal.
92–101	You have the basic climbing skills you need; you must now concentrate on honing those skills to perfection.	51–59	Your will, vision, and positive influence have helped you lead your team upwards, to the snow line.
75–91	As you ascend the first slopes you practice your climbing skills, striving to develop and refine these crucial capabilities.	42–50	You are on the move up the trail, helping your team members move in the right direction.
25–74	At the base camp your first efforts must center on practicing the skills you will need if you are to reach the peak.	15–41	You are at the base camp making plans to begin your ascent.

Visionary Culture Building Scores

Range	Interpretation
48–50	You have successfully reached the peak of your mountain by enlisting the energies of others who have come to believe in your vision.
43–47	You are on the final ascent; everyone on your team can see their goal ahead.
37–42	At the snow line your energies must go into the continuing effort to unify the team to attain the summit.
29–36	On the trail up you are constantly engaged in establishing the team's common goals.
10–28	At the base camp in the foothills your challenge is to form the individual climbers into a real team.

Interpreting Your Scoring Pattern

It might seem natural to expect your three scores to be all high, all moderate, or all low. However, such consistency is not always the case. Most of us have areas of strength as well as areas in which further development is warranted. You can identify such areas by examining the three major subscores: Visionary Leadership Behavior, Visionary Leadership Characteristics, and Visionary Culture Building. Refer back to the two triangles on page 11, on which you plotted your Self and Others Average subscores. Recall that you connected the three points in each triangle, forming a smaller triangle within the larger one. The larger the triangle that is created by your personal data, the stronger is your overall visionary leadership pattern.

Look to see whether one or more of these subscores, on one or both triangle displays, are especially strong or weak. When one or two of the scores are stronger than the other(s), you can see easily the area(s) in which further development is needed. Examples of patterns that emphasize one or two of the three dimensions of visionary leadership were illustrated on pages 12, 13, and 14.

Your visionary leadership pattern can help you to focus on the area(s) of visionary leadership that you might wish to explore in depth. The way to do this is to first identify the area (Behavior, Characteristics, or Culture Building) in which your score was lowest. Then examine the specific *LBQ* scales in that area, to see whether your score on one or another of these scales was exceptionally low. If so, you have identified a specific area for development.

On the following pages you will find, first, some guidelines to help you determine what is a high or a low score. Next are brief but specific discussions of each of the ten *LBQ* scales. Finally, some advice is offered on how you might begin to construct your own visionary leadership development plan.

Focusing On Specific Areas of Strength and Challenge

Your scores are the result of your responses (and those of your associates) to the fifty statements that assess your own visionary leadership. The *LBQ* has ten scales, each made up of five statements, so that for each scale the score can be as low as five or as high as twenty–five. The fifty statements measure the extent to which you engage in certain actions, possess certain characteristics, or affect the organization's culture in ways related to visionary leadership.

Examine carefully your responses and those of your associates on each of the ten scales. This will provide you with valuable information about your leadership style and the effects of that style on others and on the organization as a whole.

Of course, a high or low score on any one of the fifty specific statements does not necessarily imply effective or ineffective leadership. To explore your scores in a meaningful way, you first determined your overall score and your three major subscores. You could then see how you compare with several hundred of the more than 100,000 managers who have completed the *LBQ*. You were also able to see whether your associates perceive you differently from the way you see yourself. Thus you should now have a good, overall picture of yourself from the perspective of Visionary Leadership Theory.

Your *LBQ* data will, however, be even more useful to you if you examine your scores on the ten specific scales. Look for high or low scores — Self or Other — on particular scales, using the following rough guidelines:

Very High	23–25
High	21–22
Average	18–20
Low	16–17
Very Low	5–15

You can identify specific scales that you might want to work on to improve your scores. You can also find areas of strength that you might capitalize on or use to greater positive effect. A review of the comments below for those scales on which you show especially high or low scores may assist you in your efforts.

Visionary Leadership Behavior Scores

Scale 1: *Clear Leadership* (Items 1, 11, 21, 31, 41)

Bennis found that exceptional executives pay especially close attention to people with whom they communicate. They focus on the key issues under discussion and help others to see these issues clearly. They understand the relative importance or priorities of different issues under discussion and concentrate only on the most important issues. Overall, this factor comes together as the ability to manage one's attention and to direct the attention of others.

Scale 2: *Communicative Leadership* (Items 2, 12, 22, 32, 42)

This is a closely interrelated set of statements that center on the leader's interpersonal communication skills. This includes the ability to get the meaning of a message across, even if this means devising some innovative way to ensure that the idea is understood. Also included is attention to and appreciation for feelings, both one's own and those of others.

Scale 3: *Consistent Leadership* (Items 3, 13, 23, 33, 43)

The key factor here is the leader's perceived trustworthiness. Leaders demonstrate this by their willingness to take clear positions, by avoiding "flip–flop" shifts in position, and by following through on commitments. These actions show that the leader is reliable, and can therefore be trusted to do what has been promised.

Scale 4: *Caring Leadership* (Items 4, 14, 24, 34, 44)

This scale concerns the way the leader treats others (and him- or herself, too) in daily interactions. That is, the visionary leader consistently and constantly expresses concern and care for others and their feelings. High self-regard is also characteristic of visionary leaders, who typically have positive feelings about themselves. They exhibit self-respect, as well as respect for others. Underlying such positive regard for self and others is the leader's clear sense of how he or she fits into the organization, both now and in the future.

Scale 5: *Creative Leadership* (Items 5, 15, 25, 35, 45)

Visionary leaders don't spend a lot of time and energy on plans to protect themselves against failure (a "CYA" approach). While they may at first glance appear to be risk takers, this is not really the case. That is, after first determining what must be done to ensure success, all their energy is invested in actions designed around their plans. The risks they take are, in their own view, not really risks. This is because visionary leaders are confident that they can do what is required in order to achieve what they see as possible. Perhaps most important of all, visionary leaders design and create challenging opportunities that others can buy into and feel a sense of ownership about. In this way, followers help create a shared vision.

Visionary Leadership Characteristics Scores

Scale 6: *Confident Leadership* (Items 6, 16, 26, 36, 46)

Effective visionary leaders have a basic sense of self-assurance, an underlying belief that they can personally make a difference and have an impact on people, events, and organizational achievements. They believe, in other words, that they can have an effect on both actions and outcomes. They know that they can make a difference.

Scale 7: *Empowered Leadership* (Items 7, 17, 27, 37, 47)

Leaders have a strong need for power and influence; this should not be surprising. But visionary leaders don't want power and influence just because they enjoy the status of giving orders and being obeyed. Rather, they know that it is through power and influence that productive action is directed toward achieving organizational goals. What's more, they realize that power and influence must be widely shared, not just exerted at the top levels by a few. In effective organizations, everyone feels he or she has a lot of influence, especially over the job for which one is personally responsible. Effective visionary leaders use power to empower others, who can then use their power and influence to help construct a shared vision.

Scale 8: *Visionary Leadership* (Items 8, 18, 28, 38, 48)

It is from the factor assessed by this scale that we derive the term "visionary leadership." Visionary leaders are able to think clearly over relatively long spans of time, at least a few years. Their visions, and the more specific goals along the way, are not based on short-term "to do" lists but are conditions that they are committed to creating over the long term. They know what actions must be taken to stay on the right track. They are able to explain clearly their long-range views to others, at least in basic outline, so that followers not only become committed to a vision but become active in defining and constructing that vision. Visionary leaders see how their plans can be extended across larger and larger segments of the organization, thus adding value to a larger part of the system. Finally, they can conceive of how their visions might be expanded beyond their current views and plans, to include the contributions of others.

Visionary Culture Building Scales

Scale 9: *Organizational Leadership* (Items 9, 19, 29, 39, 49)

All organizations must deal with change, achieve goals, coordinate the activities of the organization's members, and maintain a strong culture of shared values, beliefs, and assumptions. This scale examines the degree to which the leader has a positive impact on these matters, helping the organization to adapt more effectively, to attain goals, to get members to work together cooperatively in teams and between teams, and to maintain a strong set of shared values and beliefs. To the extent that visionary leaders can do these things they help to improve organizational functioning, thus laying the foundation for their visions.

Scale 10: *Cultural Leadership* (Items 10, 20, 30, 40, 50)

An organization's culture is defined by the stable set of assumptions, beliefs, and values shared by its members. Some values, beliefs, and assumptions are more likely than others to support effective functioning and the implementation of an organizational vision. This scale measures the extent to which the leader is able to develop or inculcate values that will strengthen organizational functioning — managing change, achieving goals, coordinating teamwork, and maintaining the culture — and, at the same time, help build and support an organizational vision.

Some Food for Thought

The information you get from the *LBQ* can be used to analyze and modify your own visionary leadership behaviors, to develop further those personal characteristics associated with effective visionary leadership, and to consider how you might go about improving your organization's culture. The three *LBQ* scores, and the specific scales of which they are composed, can help you develop an organizatonal vision and begin work to make it a reality.

Very few people score exceptionally high in all three visionary leadership areas or on most or all of the ten scales. Nonetheless, if they are to be effective, all leaders must act, to some degree, in the ways identified here. Moreover, it really is a matter of degree, not of "having it" or "not having it." Low scores are guideposts for action, not signs of failure. Both high *and* low scores can be "good." High scores help identify areas of strength, areas one might better use. Low scores are indicators of an opportunity for improvement.

Some things are harder to change than others. Most of us find it easier to learn new behaviors than to learn to accept different ways of looking at things, for example, changing our attitudes about power and influence. But it is a matter of degree. Small changes and improvements can make real differences! The following suggestions may prove helpful, for your individual consideration or for group discussion:

- Take one of the ten visionary leadership scales on which your score was relatively high. Can you identify specific examples of your own behavior that illustrate this scale? Can you identify circumstances in which you might use that behavior but are not doing so now?

- Consider a visionary leadership scale on which your score was relatively low. Outline one or two specific situations that you will be in during the next week or so, in which you could take the opportunity to display different behavior, exhibit a different characteristic approach, or take different strategic actions to contribute to effectiveness or instill positive values. Identify some specific and detailed examples of what you might do.

- Do you think that leaders of major organizations or political leaders exhibit the behaviors, characteristics, or strategic actions measured by the *LBQ*? Can you identify some specific examples?

Bibliography

Bernard M. Bass. *Leadership and Performance Beyond Expectations.* New York: Free Press, 1985.

Warren Bennis and Burt Nanus. *Leaders: The Strategies for Taking Charge.* New York: Harper & Row, 1985.

James McGregor Burns. *Leadership.* New York: Harper & Row, 1978.

Paul Hersey and Kenneth H. Blanchard. *Management of Organizational Behavior (6th ed.)* Englewood Cliffs, NJ: Prentice-Hall, 1992.

James Kouzes and Barry Z. Posner. *The Leadership Challenge.* San Francisco: Jossey-Bass, 1985.

David C. McClelland and David H. Burnham. "Power is the Great Motivator." *Harvard Business Review,* Jan./Feb. 1976, pages 100–110.

Talcott Parsons. *Structure and Process in Modern Societies.* New York: Free Press, 1960.

Edgar H. Schein. *Organizational Culture and Leadership* *(2nd ed.)* San Francisco: Jossey-Bass, 1992.

Suggested Reading

The best general reader on leadership is *Contemporary Issues in Leadership (3rd ed.),* by William E. Rosenbach and Robert Taylor (Boulder, CO: Westview Press, 1993). Marshall Sashkin and Herbert J. Walberg edited an exceptionally clear volume of research reports on leadership in educational organizations, *Educational Leadership and School Culture,* (Berkeley, CA: McCutchan, 1992). To read more about Marshall Sashkin's Visionary Leadership Theory, see the booklets *Becoming A Visionary Leader* and *A New Vision of Leadership,* both available from HRD Press.

Management Development

Some of the most useful tools for management development are the Situational Leadership instruments and related materials developed by Dr. Paul Hersey and available from HRD Press. Situational Leadership provides a sophisticated approach for teaching and learning sound management concepts and skills, a necessary foundation for visionary leadership.

About the Author

Marshall Sashkin is professor of human resource development at The George Washington University in Washington, DC, where he teaches graduate courses in the area of management and organization development, leadership, consulting skills, and research design and method. Marshall received his bachelors degree in psychology from the University of California, Los Angeles, and earned a Ph.D. in organizational psychology from the University of Michigan. He has conducted research, taught at several universities, and consulted with numerous public and private sector organizations, including the Army War College, TRW, GE, and American Express. From 1979 to 1984 he was professor of industrial and organizational psychology at the University of Maryland. He served nine years as a senior associate in the Office of Educational Research and Improvement, the research application arm of the U.S. Department of Education, where he developed and guided applied research aimed at improving the organization and management of schools. Marshall has authored or co–authored more than fifty research reports and over a dozen books. One of his most recent books is *Putting Total Quality Management to Work* (with Kenneth J. Kiser; Berrett–Koehler Publishers, San Francisco, 1993). He is also author of many questionnaire instruments widely used in both research and executive development programs, including *The Visionary Leader (Leader Behavior Questionnaire), Conflict Style Inventory,* and the *MbM Questionnaire (Managing by Motivation),* all of which are published by and available from **HRD Press.**